HISTORY OF
ST. JOHN THE BAPTIST

Pseudo-Mark the Evangelist

Translated by: Francois Nau, D.P. Curtin

Copyright @ 2019 Dalcassian Press

All rights reserved. No part of this publication may be reproduced, distributed, or transmitted in any form or by any means, including photocopying, recording, or other electronic or mechanical methods, without the prior written permission of the publisher, except in the case of brief quotations embodied in critical reviews and certain other non-commercial uses permitted by copyright law. For permission request, write to Dalcassian Press at dalcassianpublishing at gmail.com

ISBN: 979-8-3302-6685-2 (Paperback)

Library of Congress Control Number:
Author: Curtin, D.P. (1985-)

Printed by Ingram Content Group, 1 Ingram Blvd, La Vergne, Tennessee

First printing edition 2019.

HISTORY OF ST. JOHN THE BAPTIST
MARTYRDOM, THAT IS, THE BIRTH AND BEHEADING OF SAINT JOHN THE BAPTIST

Attributed to: St. Mark the Evangelist
Translated into French by: Fr. Francois Nau

I. HIS BIRTH. When five thousand five hundred years minus six months had passed since the creation of the world, Saint John the Baptist was born, according to the prediction of the Holy Spirit, the fulfillment of the Law and the Prophets, the herald and precursor of Our Lord Jesus Christ the Son of God. Immediately filled with the Holy Spirit, he went into the desert. He lived in the desert, eating locusts, wild honey, and the juice of plants, until the day of his manifestation to Israel.

II. HIS VOCATION. At the moment when he was eating herbs, the archangel Gabriel appeared to him and said, "This is what the Lord God says, the One who formed you from your mother's womb and marked you for the salvation and instruction of men: Go into the inhabited places and baptize all those who come to you to repent; behold, I will send my only Son to deliver all men from every diabolical error. While you baptize men, tell them: Repent, for the kingdom of heaven is near. My Son himself will come to you and be baptized by you to sanctify the waters, and all those who come after will be sanctified in them. Here is the sign that will be given to you, so that you know that he is my Son: you will see the Spirit descend in the form of a dove and (He) upon whom you remain, that One is the judge of the living and the dead who must deliver from all divine wrath those who believe in him."

III. HIS MINISTRY. John went to Elim and baptized there. All the Jews came to him and were baptized. However, many were scandalized on occasion by him and did not believe in his preaching. He said to the Jews that he was baptizing, "Brood of vipers! Who warned you to flee from the coming wrath? Produce fruit in keeping with repentance. And John wore clothing made of camel's hair and had a leather belt around his waist. His fame spread throughout Galilee and Judea, and many people came to him. Forty disciples gathered around him and followed him.

IV. RELATIONSHIP WITH HEROD. Herod, the very impious tyrant, ruled over Judea. One of his officials went to John, where he was baptizing, heard his words, and then reported everything to Herod. When Herod heard about John and the teachings he was spreading, he said, "After many years, a prophet has appeared again (in Israel), a scandal to men. By my power! I am very pleased with this news, I want to bring him before my authority, as I have some questions to ask him."

The second of Herod, answered and said to King Herod: "We beg your divinity, O master, to bring him to this city, so that we may all learn what he says and does."
King Herod lived in the city of Sebaste. King Herod then called Berinos, the captain of fifty, and said to him: "Go to the land of the Jordan and bring me here both John and his forty disciples."

The captain of fifty went and came to the place where John was baptizing. When he saw him, along with all those who were with him and the glory that covered his face, he was filled with fear and dared not speak to him.
John, seeing that he was afraid and knowing why he had been sent, said to him: "Go tell King Herod: It is not yet time for me to appear before you. There will come days when I will present myself before you; I will rebuke your impieties and show you the transgression of the law that you have committed; for your spirit is evil and the thought of your soul is bitter; you have not been satisfied by the debaucheries that surround you, but you have dilated strangely and you are even preparing to climb onto your brother's bed. You do not see God who knows everything, He who gave you the kingdom, because you have denied Him, and you have abandoned the Creator of the universe. You say in your criminal heart: I am and there is no other. But here comes He who is to come and he will not delay." The leader of fifty returned, came near to Herod and reported to him everything that John had said. Herod, at these words, was astonished and said to his nobles: What is the spirit that animates this fatal man, that he revealed to me first, although absent, the plan of my mind, and that nothing escapes him! I am very struck by this." Since then, Herod was thinking of killing John and wanted to do so.

V. BAPTISM OF CHRIST. Now John learned from Our Lord Jesus Christ that he had come and was staying near the Jordan River - for that is where he was supposed to come to be baptized by him. After thirty days, Jesus came to the Jordan River and when John saw him coming towards him, he stretched out his hands as well as the cloak he was wearing and said to those who were there around him: "Here is the Lamb of God, who takes away the sins of the world." Jesus came to be baptized by John and when John saw him taking the lead for this, he said to him: "It is I who need to be baptized by you and you come to me." But Jesus said to him: "Let me do it only, for it is right to fulfill all that is just." John baptized him immediately and saw the Spirit of God descending like a dove and remaining on him. And when he came out of the water, John let him go.

VI. JOHN APPEARS BEFORE HEROD. After baptizing Our Lord Jesus Christ, John went to Sebaste. Herod, hearing about it, had him brought before him. John, appearing before him and the nobles who were with him, said to him: "Why have you brought a foreign servant, especially with the confidence you have in your own vanity? Why do you fear that the light will separate from the darkness? Why do you hide the poison and the worm that are in your wicked heart?" Have you gone and wickedly defiled your brother's bed? Why do you show yourself as strong and calm on the outside, while inside your heart is troubled by adultery? Why do you surround yourself with piety when you are consumed by licentiousness? It is not permitted for you to have your brother's wife."

VII. HIS IMPRISONMENT. Upon hearing these words, Herod, seized with great anger for being rebuked in front of everyone, ordered him to be thrown into prison in chains. But all those who had heard John's words and seen him went to the prison. Herod, learning that numerous crowds were coming to the prison and that there was much murmuring in the city about John, thought of putting him to death soon. John asked the prison guard to let his disciples come to him, but the guard refused, fearing Herod. When the disciples arrived, the prison guard stopped them from approaching him. But John asked the guard again, and he let them in. His disciples greeted him and wept aloud, but the guard entered and told them to be quiet. As the evening approached, we began to pray, and then (John) kissed each of us and started to pray in these words:

> *"O God, who exists before all ages with your Word, our God, who has filled us with the Holy Spirit, who has solidified the heavens, founded the earth, and arranged hidden beds for the*

waters of the sky, who has appointed multitudes of Angels to govern according to order, who has set limits to the sea and does not allow it to rise against us in a disorderly manner, but compels it to obey men, who commands the waters to produce living creatures and to whom everything obeys, also give to your servants here present to believe in your presence in your Christ who has made all things, visible and invisible, do not turn away, do not leave us, do not distance yourself from us, and do not be angry with us, but save us, you who are the port without storm and the good pilot, for to you is the glory forever and ever. Amen."

After this prayer, he said to them, "I want you to know, my children, that tomorrow, at the sixth hour, Herod will send a soldier to cut off my head and bring it to him as a dessert on a plate in the palace during his meal, in front of all those who are seated with him; he will give it to a girl as a reward for her dance and she will give it to her mother because of her bad behavior and the blame I have addressed to Herod. I implore you not to abandon my teachings, not to be afraid when I am put to death; do not hate the (executioners), do not walk with unruly men, do not speak ill of your brothers. Do not let the fear of men separate you from Christ, accept death and do not deny Christ: leave the cities and keep his faith; give up riches and love only him; let yourself be struck for him and do not strike; seek him and do not let your soul drift away from him; stay away from all theft; turn your faces away from adultery; spit in the face of fornication and greed; remove pride from your home.

"Remember the prophets of the Mosaic law; let your soul be diligent and your heart take flight towards God; let your torch burn; let your lamps shine; let your mouth sing hymns; let your sacrifices not be corrupted; let your speech be seasoned with salt (of prudence)." Then he gave them peace again, embraced them a third time, and sent them away.

VIII. HEROD'S FEAST. The next day was Herod's feast day, and Herod called all his nobles to the banquet. The guests were: Nil the second of Herod; Cyril the third; Lucius the fourth; Hygnos the fifth; Acholios the sixth; Caius the seventh; Felix the eighth; Sosipatros the ninth; Anthony the tenth; Achilles the eleventh; Alypius the twelfth; Iras the thirteenth; Alaphios the fourteenth; Prochorus the fifteenth; Hemerius the sixteenth; Africanus the seventeenth; Julian the eighteenth; Tranquillianus the nineteenth; another Herod the twentieth; another Julian the twenty-first; and Aetius the twenty-second."

Such are the princes of King Herod, such are those who were invited to his feast. The day before, Herod was inflamed with passion for Herodias and the demon, who everywhere and always introduces evil through weak women, set his sights on this person to carry out injustice on Herod's birthday.

When the nobles came before their king, they began to praise him and say, "The soul of all your children wanted to rejoice in the happiness of your piety, our terrified enemies suddenly vanished and ended in perdition; our strength, supported by you, is increased by the kindness that flows from you to all your subjects.

However, O victorious king, let your servants not sit down to the meal until John is either freed or put to death, for he has destroyed our hope and caused harm and loss to us: when we had placed. Our hope in your divinity, he brought another law and said that there was another Christ and king. If such a law prevails, our doctrines will be destroyed and our forces will be reduced to impotence. But have him interrogated: if he stops this vain teaching, let him be released, and if he does not stop, let him be put to death." The king sent Julien and told him, "Question John, learn about him, gather his words and let me know, but hurry before we sit down for dinner."

Julien went to the prison and said to John, "Why have you been thrown into prison?" John replied, "Because I have criticized the impiety of your master." Julien replied and said to him, "You would have been better off not repeating that to me." John said, "I said that in front of your master and you tell me not to repeat it in front of you!" Julien said to him, "Stop, John, this rebellious attitude and do not force the kings or rather the gods to take action against you." John replied, "I was sent to condemn injustice." Julien replied, "We do not have to take care of talkative spirits, stop dogmatizing." Saint John replied: "Go to your master and tell him that John condemns what he is doing and that his kingdom is but vanity." Julien, upon hearing these words, went to report them to King Herod, and he fell silent, for it was already time for the meal.

IX. DEATH OF JOHN. When they were at the table and had eaten, they became drunk and lost all human respect; then Herod brought in the daughter of Herodias to dance before him. She entered and did not want to dance. The king said to her, "Ask me for anything up to half my kingdom, and I will do it for you."

So she danced and pleased Herod and his guests, then she went out and said to her mother, "What should I ask the king for?" Her mother said to her, "Ask for the head of John the Baptist."

So Herodias entered and said to the king, "Give me on this platter the head of John the Baptist, and that will be enough for me."

Herod was distressed because he wanted to speak with John face to face, but because of his oath and his guests, he did not want to refuse her. He called a servant and said to him, "Go to the prison, behead John, put his head on a platter and bring it to me." The servant went, cut off the head of Saint John, put it on a platter, and brought it to Herod. Herod took it and gave it to the young girl. She, receiving it, danced with it in the middle of the banquet hall and gave it to her mother, Herodias.

X. HIS BURIAL. Acholios, one of Herod's guests, was a disciple of Saint John, and he was dear to Herodias' mother; so he left the meal and went to ask for the head of Saint John. He received it, and as he had a brand new pitcher in which he had not yet put anything, he placed the revered head in it, then sealed it with lead. He then called certain disciples of Saint John, six in number, and said to them, "Take the head of your master, go far from this city, and lay it down as it is in this ewer. The others will go to the prison to take the body of the holy prophet and bury it."

The six disciples of Saint John then took his head and went to the city of Emesa, located near the Saracens; they found a cave and placed the ewer containing the head of Saint John in it, and his six disciples remained there until their death.

As for me, who has written this, my brothers, I am a sinful disciple of John, I followed him and learned from him to believe in Our Lord Jesus Christ who will deliver us from future punishment."

Saint John, when he was beheaded, was thirty-three years old. He was put to death on the 29th of the month of Dystros", so we commemorate him at this moment so that we may share with him in the kingdom of heaven through Our Lord Jesus Christ to whom, with the Father and the Holy Spirit, be glory, power, honor, and adoration, now and forever and ever. Amen.

The Scriptorium Project is the work of a small group of lay people of various apostolic churches who are interested in the preservation, transmission, and translation of the works of the early and medieval church. Our efforts are to make the works of the church fathers accessible to anyone who might have an interest in Christian antiquities and the theological, philosophical, and moral writings that have become the bedrock of Western Civilization.

To-date, our releases have pulled from the Greek, Syriac, Georgian, Latin, Celtic, Ethiopian, and Coptic traditions of Christianity, and have been pulled from sundry local traditions and languages.

www.ingramcontent.com/pod-product-compliance
Lightning Source LLC
LaVergne TN
LVHW061044070526
838201LV00073B/5180